The Zeppelin Offensive

A German Perspective in Pictures and Postcards

David Marks

AIR WORLD

First published in Great Britain in 2019 by
Air World
An imprint of
Pen & Sword Books Ltd
Yorkshire – Philadelphia

Copyright © David Marks 2019

ISBN 978 1 52673 719 9

A CIP catalogue record for this book is
available from the British Library.

Printed and bound in India by Replika Press Pvt. Ltd.

Pen & Sword Books Limited incorporates the imprints of Atlas, Archaeology,
Aviation, Discovery, Family History, Fiction, History, Maritime, Military, Military
Classics, Politics, Select, Transport, True Crime, Air World, Frontline Publishing,
Leo Cooper, Remember When, Seaforth Publishing, The Praetorian Press,
Wharncliffe Local History, Wharncliffe Transport, Wharncliffe True Crime
and White Owl.

For a complete list of Pen & Sword titles please contact

PEN & SWORD BOOKS LIMITED
47 Church Street, Barnsley, South Yorkshire, S70 2AS, England
E-mail: enquiries@pen-and-sword.co.uk
Website: www.pen-and-sword.co.uk

Or

PEN AND SWORD BOOKS
1950 Lawrence Rd, Havertown, PA 19083, USA
E-mail: Uspen-and-sword@casematepublishers.com
Website: www.penandswordbooks.com

Contents

Acknowledgements

Considering the development and impact of the Zeppelin raids on Britain during the First World War from the German perspective has been a fascinating task, challenging many preconceptions and allowing me to delve into that country's political climate at the time. In order to reacquaint myself with German language I even dug out and consulted my *Collins Gem German Dictionary* that I used for my O Level German studies! I have learned so much during my research and there are many postcards with interesting stories that I have had to leave aside, hopefully for another day.

As I will go to the pains of explaining in the text, this book would not have turned out as I would have liked without Mick Forsyth's skills as a translator as well as his wise counsel and suggestions. I hope he will accept both my thanks and apologies for stretching his rhyming abilities to the limit. The *Postcard Album* (http://www.tpa–project.info) has been my 'go-to' website to identify and research long gone German postcard printers and publishers and its creator, Helmfried Luers, has been of great assistance.

Ian Castle is building a formidable reputation as the leading 'First Blitz' expert, taking over that mantle from the likes of Douglas H. Robinson and Ray Rimell. Ian has been generous in his guidance and support as I worked on this book and, indeed, during all of my other Zeppelin-based endeavours. We share information and images and can talk for hours about individual raids or the smallest bomb fragment or piece of wire.

Thanks also go to 'Airship Evangelist' Giles Camplin as his sterling work on behalf of the Airship Heritage Trust and the Airship Association remains an inspiration. Also 'mentioned in despatches' are my pals from the Great War Forum for their encouragement and to thank them for the many convivial evenings we have shared at The Pineapple.

Last, but by no means least, a big thank you to my family and to my closest friends, Nick Nicola, Marco Barbuti and Lakis Pavlou, for putting up with my acute case of 'Zeppelinitis', and to the partners and staff of David Rubin & Partners and my long-suffering boss, Paul Appleton.

David Marks
February 2019

Introduction

A s an avid postcard collector for many years, I have come to view the First World War through the prism of this simple means of communication. The significant role that the picture postcard played during the conflict has yet to be fully appreciated by historians and the public alike. In particular, the postcard as a propaganda tool, as used by all of the major combatants, is worthy of further study. Postcards were the social currency of the war and the language through which the soldier at the front and his people at home communicated.[1] However, in its most sophisticated form, the postcard could also be directed against both enemy and neutral countries.

In Germany, the excellent printing processes and a freer commercial climate had heralded the rapid development of the postcard prior to the outbreak of the war. In the United Kingdom, the postcard collecting craze, which had started in the Edwardian era, continued and millions of cards were acquired not only for posting, but to be added to personal collections or given as gifts. The sheer volume of postcards in circulation was staggering, and, by 1917, over 4,000 men engaged by the British forces postal services were handling around two million letters and postcards a day.

I gradually moved away from collecting British humorous and patriotic postcards as I became captivated by the quality of the artwork of their German counterparts. There were many similarities in the depictions of the respective home fronts, with artist-drawn and comic postcards showing soldiers in training, on leave or returning home wounded, and women taking men's roles in the workplace. They shared similar jokes and human touches, which, interestingly, extended to postcards making light of food shortages and rationing for propaganda purposes.

The approach that German postcard publishers brought to their patriotic offerings was unsurprising. By featuring the widespread use of Iron Crosses and Teutonic images, these helped to reinforce a national identity, as did the use of royalty and military leaders. For example, Field Marshal Hindenburg could be seen as an almost

---

1. Laffin, *World War I in Postcards*, p.2.

Germany's Pride: Kaiser Wilhelm II and Paul von Hindenburg in a dramatic pose. A charity postcard for the Red Cross Association. (*Pub. Rotophot A.-G., Berlin*)

I AM KITCHENER CALLED "K. OF K."
AND MY ORDERS YOU ALL MUST OBEY,
AS THE KING IS MY MASTER,
IF YOU DON'T ENLIST FASTER,
PERHAPS I MAY FORCE YOU ONE DAY.

In England, postcards of Field Marshal Kitchener were equally common and imposing.

A patriotic German dachshund makes its disdain for captured enemy ordnance clear. (*Pub. Albert Fink, Berlin*)

This poor dachshund, representing the German army, has been soundly beaten. The Teutonic associations of the dachshund resulted in a decline in its popularity as a breed in Britain. (*Pub. A. M. Davis & Co, London*)

direct counterpart for the equally formidable Lord Kitchener. The personifications of both countries were also well represented through images of John Bull and Der Deutsche Michel (the German Michael) and, of course, the ubiquitous bulldog or dachshund. However, I was not prepared for the satirical and, at times, scatological humour employed by German artists and their publishers, which often carried deeper political meanings than in Britain and, generally, displayed a more heavy-handed approach in their mockery of their opponents. One theme was used again and again in these postcards: the emblematic power of the Zeppelin airship and its inventor, Ferdinand Adolf Heinrich August Graf von Zeppelin.

In my debut book, *Let the Zeppelins Come*, which was published in March 2017 by Amberley Publishing, I considered the impact of Germany's unprecedented aerial bombing campaign against Britain and how the postcard was used to rally civilian morale. The message was clear; the population was not going to be intimidated by the Zeppelin menace, despite finding itself under aerial attack for the first time. A remarkable resilience shines through in these postcards and, once the raiders had been overcome, their tone became triumphant with the pilots, who were responsible for bringing down 'the Baby Killers', becoming heroes in their own right. In this book, I consider how Count Zeppelin's invention formed an integral part of Germany's wartime identity. Whilst the public's expectations were, in reality, in stark contrast to the Zeppelin's actual military capabilities, it did not disappoint as a psychological weapon.

In contrast to the narrative of the British 'Zeppelin' postcard, which can be summed up as 'We are not defeated – we are not afraid', the German offerings tell a different story, being the culmination of a nationalistic culture that had developed in the pre-war years. The postcards and propaganda are not all about Wagnerian imagery, but also include images that are rich in humour and with a strong satirical edge.

In Jerome K. Jerome's 1889 novel, *Three Men in a Boat*, and its sequel *Three Men on the Bummel*, the narrator remarks on the popular notion that the Germans 'hadn't any sense of humour'. The following pages may help to dispel that notion.

Typical examples showing the resilience of the British public in the face of the Zeppelin menace. Both postcards published by the prolific firm of *Bamforth & Co., Holmfirth*.

These raiders make you feel very unsettled—if they dropped a bomb here they'd blow this screen to smithereens!

A Note on Methodology and Translations

As with *Let the Zeppelins Come*, every postcard, picture or other artefact in this book is taken from my own collection and, if there are any glaring omissions, it is simply because I have been unable to source or acquire them. The book is a mixture of a chronological narrative, where the postcards are shown as depicting key events, and an exploration of the themes that illustrate how the Zeppelin was portrayed by Germany for its propaganda purposes.

Many of the postcards and other objects in this book are accompanied by short rhyming verses and phrases, often incorporating references to historic and current events, as well as myths, legends and local colloquialisms. Part of the fun initially but, latterly, a cause of great frustration, was to try to translate these verses and phrases effectively. In addition, the images themselves often contain hidden meanings, which need to be interpreted to enable the reader to appreciate fully the message being communicated to the German public.

At this point, I must express my gratitude to translator extraordinaire, Michael Forsyth. I met Mick through the Great War Forum and his help in translating these postcards has been invaluable. As I quickly found out to my cost, Google Translate could not achieve the results I was looking for!

The problem is that the original text is often extremely contrived in order to compose a ditty that rhymes, so it is not written in 'natural' German from the start. Of course, the copywriter, who may or may not have been the cartoonist, has a completely free choice of words and phrases, which gives him much more latitude than the translator, who is obliged to try and reflect the flavour of the original and, if possible, produce something that sounds, more or less, reasonable and, at least sort of, rhymes.

As Mick explained to me, it's like translating a Latin motto, where the English rendering is often very free compared with the literal meaning of the rather Spartan Latin wording. The same principle applies to here, but you can only go so far to 'improve' the literal rendering before it ceases to be a translation at all.

In the majority of cases I have used Mick's translations, but readers should note that the ultimate decision as to each translation and the interpretation of the postcards themselves in the book rests solely with the author. It is a fact that some of the translations will be better than others, but the supreme irony is that one or two of them have gone into rhyming English relatively well and a critical reader will doubtless ask 'If you can get these ones to work, why can't you do the same for all the others?'

I would, of course, be delighted to hear from any reader with their comments on the translations used and my interpretation of the images.

Chapter One

'Zeppelin Kommt!'

G ermany is the true home of the airship and Count Zeppelin's influence on the design of the large rigid airship is undisputed. The inventor and his airships were seen as a blessing of the modern age and a manifestation of the technological sublime and his invention belonged to the German public.[1] It fired their imagination and Zeppelins were a source of pride, fascination and wonder. Kaiser Wilhelm II was a devotee, calling the Count 'the greatest German of the twentieth century'.

The German Aerial Transport Company, DELAG, the acronym for *Deutsche Luftschiffahrts-Aktiengesellschaft*, was the world's first airline to use an aircraft in

Friedrichshafen 10 November 1908. Kaiser Wilhelm, after witnessing a splendid series of manoeuvres by Zeppelin's eponymous airship, personally conferred upon the Count the Order of the Black Eagle, the highest Prussian decoration.

1. de Syon, *Zeppelin! Germany and the Airship , 1900–1939* , p.39.

Berlin 29 August 1909. The Kaiser greets Count Zeppelin on landing. 'Countless thousands of Berliners, in the last stage of Zeppelin dementia, cheered themselves hoarse', reported the *Daily Mail*.

revenue service. It was founded in 16 November 1909 and operated Zeppelin airships. Commencing operations on 19 June 1910, DELAG had the proud record of having safely carried over 10,000 paying passengers, travelling in comfort with wicker chairs, a viewing gondola, cold buffets and wines.

Due to the development of these commercial airships, nearly everybody in Germany had seen a Zeppelin in flight during its four years of peacetime operations. Even though they could not afford trips costing more than a month's average wage, they cheered the spectacle from below and 'Zeppelin Kommt!' became a nationwide chorus of anticipation and excitement. The craze for all things 'Zeppelin' spread rapidly and was, remarkably, immune to a succession of major accidents in 1910 and 1911 to three DELAG ships.

The German military showed an interest in this developing technology and agreed to purchase an airship if it could reach certain criteria, including a continuous journey of twenty-four hours. Once this requirement had been achieved in 1909, the army purchased two of the Count's airships, *LZ3* and *LZ5*. Further orders followed and the navy also took an interest and purchased its own airships. Rival company, *Luftschiffbau Schütte-Lanz*, with its wooden construction, as opposed to the Zeppelin's aluminium (later duralumin) framework, was also successful

One of the highly popular Arthur Thiele series of six postcards, which depict the chaotic excitement of a visiting Zeppelin. Towns considered it a public distinction if the Zeppelin simply passed overhead. (*Pub. Adolf Klauss & Co., Leipzig*)

W. Sanke of Berlin was a prolific producer of early aviation photo-postcards. Pictured is Schütte-Lanz II, with its aerodynamically optimised hull, one of many design innovations that were soon adopted by its competitor, Zeppelin.

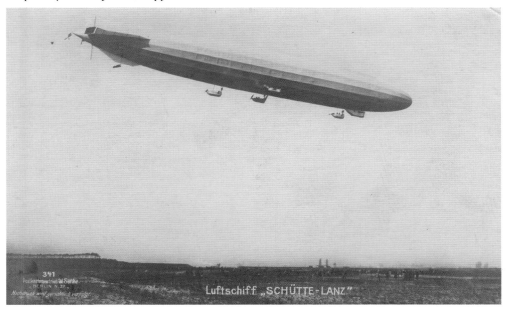

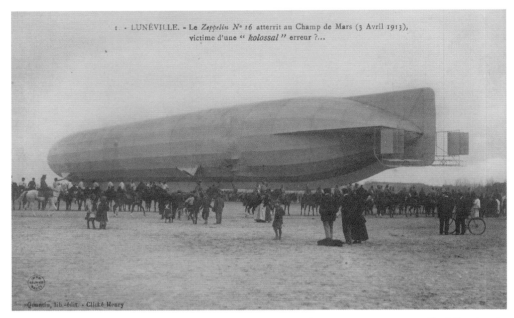

Zeppelin *Z IV* on the cavalry parade ground of the French army camp at Lunéville following its emergency landing. Was this a 'colossal' error from a 'colossal' airship? The French public believed that the Germans had deliberately provoked a diplomatic incident. (*Pub. Quantin, lib.-edit. – Cliché Henry*)

The Deutsche Michel, supported by Zeppelins, explains to the French soldier that he cannot be goaded into another war but, if he is, the outcome will be the same.

in providing two of its own airships to the army. DELAG's personnel played an important role in training army and navy flight crews before and during the war.

However, despite the variety of airships in use, they were all destined to be called Zeppelins due to the fame of their inventor and it is rare for a postcard to distinguish between airship types, particularly for propaganda purposes.

The development of the new technology for military purposes rekindled nationalistic pride, particularly given the tense Franco-German relations stemming from, amongst other things, the possession of Alsace and Lorraine. In contrast to the Anglo–German naval arms race between 1906 and 1914, the French were noted for their advances in military aviation and, whilst the emphasis was on aeroplanes, they also made great advances in semi-rigid and non-rigid dirigibles, as opposed to the German rigid-framed types. In April 1913 there was the diplomatic incident at Lunéville, where *Z IV* accidentally strayed into French territory and was forced to land in the garrison town. It heightened tensions between the countries and allowed the French to perform a detailed examination of the Zeppelin.

In 1913 the German government celebrated the centenary of the 1813–15 wars of liberation, where a series of battles were fought against Napoleon and his marshals, which freed the German states from the domination of the First French

The New Course is a political term usually synonymous with post-Bismarck Germany, but is used here to support the decision to go to war. The Kaiser is flanked by his Chief of the General Staff and his Chancellor. The Zeppelin is one of the tools at the Empire's disposal. (*Pub. Stengel & Co., Dresden*)

Our Fliers are ready for war. Part of the 'Seven War-Wonders' series. (*Pub. Hans Friedrich Abshagen, Dresden*)

Published by the Continental-Caoutchouc-und-Gutta-Percha Compagnie. The famous rubber company advertises its role in the war. A crewman, perched on a humanized observation balloon, keeps a watch on the enemy for Field Marshall Hindenburg.

Count Zeppelin's stirring quote. In 1914, he attempted to secure an appointment at the front, but the authorities decided that his true position was elsewhere.

Empire. On 18 October 1913 the massive Monument to the Battle of Nations, or *Völkerschlachtdenkmal*, was dedicated at Leipzig. The opening of a new airship station in Leipzig was staged in order to coincide with the centenary celebrations and the image of a Zeppelin flying over the *Völki*, or the new *Luftschiffhalle*, became the subject of popular postcards. It was also an opportunity to taunt the French, as the postcard shown at the bottom of page 4 demonstrates.

When war was declared, it was believed that it would only be a matter of time before the might of the Zeppelin would be unleashed against Britain. In reality, Germany possessed just eleven airships, including the three commercial Zeppelins operated by DELAG. There was just one Zeppelin under the control of the navy, with the remaining airships, to include Schütte-Lanz airship *SL2*, being operated by the army.

While new airships were being produced for the military, early offensive operations were undertaken by the existing fleet. However, this revealed a vulnerability to ground fire unless flown at high altitude and, after less than four weeks' fighting, Germany's airship strength had been reduced by almost half. Rumour and propaganda filled the void and the Zeppelin acquired a reputation quite disproportionate to its actual effectiveness.[2]

The image opposite is a fine example of how Count Zeppelin was venerated and used as a figurehead on postcards. It contrasts the pre-war joy of a Zeppelin passing over a city with the destruction caused by a fleet of Zeppelins attacking what is clearly London. The quote, attributed to Zeppelin himself, and bearing a facsimile of his signature, translates, as 'If the Zeppelins increase the strength of the Fatherland against the ring of its enemies by even the smallest amount, then my life's work has not been in vain.'

The quote neatly encapsulates the belief that Germany was fighting a defensive war and, as the following chapters demonstrate, the Zeppelin, with its command of the air and the capacity to lay waste to its enemies, became integral to the propaganda that underpins this concept.

---

2. Syon, *Zeppelin! Germany and the Airship , 1900–1939*, p.88.

Chapter Two

'Gott Strafe England!'

There seemed to be no shadow of doubt in the mind of any ordinary German I met in those days that the German people were setting out upon a war of defence…. As far as I could learn, the average German firmly believed that the war had been thrust upon Germany by the ruthless despotism of Russia and by the mad chauvinism of France. Later on all this was forgotten, and England became and remained the arch-enemy who, by her devilish diplomacy, had drawn France and Russia into her net and cleverly tricked them into war with Germany for her own base ends.

Escapes and Adventures (1928) by Wallace Ellison[1]

Ellison's quote records the prevailing public opinion that Germany was fighting a defensive war, inflicted on it as a result of military encirclement by its enemies, principally in the shape of the Franco-Russian Entente and subsequently 'England' (the term Britain, or British, was almost never used). This view feeds into the wider concept of *Burgfrieden*, literally from the medieval term meaning 'fortress peace' or 'castle peace', representing the national unity of the German people based on shared suffering in the name of survival.

Burgfrieden was used, from August 1914, to describe the political truce which the Social Democratic Party and the other political parties agreed to during the war. The concept underpins official and unofficial war propaganda between 1914 and 1916, which coincides with the rise and fall of the Zeppelin as a viable weapon of war.

Once war had been declared, the public's patriotic fervour was reflected through the mass media and easily translated itself into popular postcards that encompassed propaganda for the war effort. The representations of Zeppelins flying over the homeland on their way to a raid on England, or in support of the High Seas Fleet, would engender optimism and could even serve as a recruitment tool.

---

1. Ellison, a lecturer in Economics at Frankfurt University at the outbreak of war, was arrested in August 1914 whilst returning to England. As a British civilian, he was interned from November 1914 until his escape three years later.

To England! A fleet of Zeppelins cross the North Sea. *Deutscher Luftflottenverein* postcard published in Berlin.

A German sailor proudly waves the *Reichskriegsflagge* to wish good luck to the Zeppelin heading out on a mission. (*Pub. Wilhelm S. Schröder Nachf., Berlin*)

The Zeppelin is flying over a battleship. Note the background of oak and laurel leaves, being symbols of strength and victory. The rallying cry of 'Gott mit uns!' is reinforced with a patriotic poem imploring the public to be faithful to the flag until death. (*Pub. Wizico, Cöln am Rhein*)

The German-Austrian Circus. The smiling ringmasters crack their whips to make their enemies perform an impossible jump. It is a cruel but not untypical postcard, which reinforces the message of the Two against the Seven. (*Pub. Paul Fink, Berlin*)

'The big trouser-wash by the Crippled-Entente'. In this example of the stereotypes employed to demonstrate German superiority over its main foes, the Russian soldier is depicted as an almost sub-human figure.

Many postcards combined patriotism with an intense hatred of the enemy, which was shown through stereotypical images of Allied troops. British soldiers are usually identified as kilted Scots and it has been suggested that this was done as a sign of effeminacy. They also wear either Victorian era pillbox hats or bearskins. French soldiers, almost always sporting moustaches and goatees, are depicted as slovenly and ill-prepared. They wear the colourful traditional uniforms of the nineteenth century with conspicuous blue coats and red trousers. Russians are depicted as bearded Cossacks, who are brutish drunks.

Such caricatures of soldiers of the three *Entente* powers, often accompanied by Belgium, Japan, Montenegro and Serbia, making up what was collectively known as 'the Seven', were the subject of hateful stereotypes in Germany. They were shown on postcards in a variety of situations, usually being thrashed, kicked or beaten by their Central Powers adversaries, or simply as weak and dishevelled opposition. The implication was clear; the militarily inferior enemy could easily be defeated by the German Empire and its Austro-Hungarian ally, i.e. the 'Two against the Seven'.

There were many popular slogans aimed against the enemy, such as *Jeder Schuss ein Russ, Jeder Stoß ein Franzos and Jeder Klaps ein Japs* (Every shot a Russian, Every blow a Frenchman and Every clap a Japanese). However, there was one rallying cry reserved for the arch-enemy that became known throughout the world: *Gott Strafe England!*

Every Shot a Russian – Every Blow a Frenchman. (*Pub. Wilhelm S. Schröder Nachf., Berlin*)

Gott Strafe England is the message on the raiding Zeppelin – a charity postcard for the German School Association in Vienna. (*Pub Josef Eberle, Vien*)

A Valkyrie escorts a fleet of heroic Zeppelins on their journey to destroy England. (*Pub. Brockhaus, Leipzig*)

During the war, the Germans printed thousands of patriotic labels to be placed on envelopes. Those bearing the term Gott Strafe England were among the most popular.

Whilst the phrase *Gott mit uns* could be applied to the conduct of the conflict generally, *Gott Strafe England* (May God Punish England) and the response *Er Strafe es* (may He do so) perfectly captured the fervour of the public and attracted the attention of postcard publishers, as well as being found on shop windows, on trams and railway compartments, in cinemas and restaurants. It was the Zeppelin that was expected to mete out this divine retribution.

In his 1917 book *My Four Years in Germany*, James W. Gerard, the late ambassador to the German Imperial Court,[2] explained that the phrase seemed to be all over Germany:

---

2. James Watson Gerard (1867–1951) served as United States Ambassador to Germany prior to US involvement in the war. For a former ambassador to the country, Gerard regarded Germany with little less than loathing.

A dramatic image as the spectral figure of a sailor looms over the invading German forces. (*Pub. Bernhard Heimann, Hamburg*)

'All declarations of war accepted here'. This direct challenge reinforces the idea of a defensive war with addition of an imposing iron fist striking at Germany's enemies. The rhyme: 'The fist as ever iron-hard. That is the German way!' (*Pub. Bruno Bürger & Ottilie, Leipzig*)

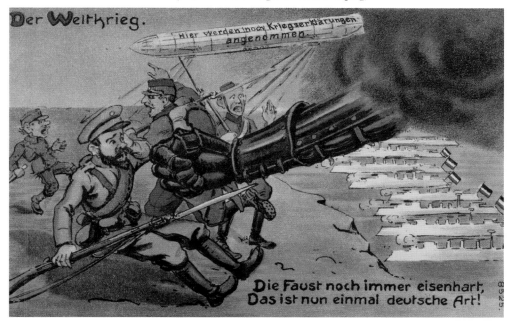

It was printed on stamps to be affixed to the back of letters like our Red Cross stamps. I even found my German body servant in the Embassy affixing these stamps to the back of all letters, official or otherwise, that were sent out. He was stopped when discovered.

After May 1915, the phrase *Gott strafe England und vernichte Italien* (God punish England and destroy Italy) became popular as did *Gott strafe das treulose Italien!* (God punish traitorous Italy). Examples of the stamps to which Gerard refers are shown on page 18.

Gerard also mentions Ernst Lissauer's 'Hymn of Hate' (*Hassgesang gegen England*), a remarkable poem, filled with Anglophobic sentiment and hatred, published in August 1914. Lissauer is also credited with coining the slogan *Gott Strafe England* and his 'Hymn of Hate' is well worth seeking out in both the original German and its English translation,[3] as it encapsulates the jingoistic wave of hysteria that gripped the country at the outbreak of the war. The closing lines of the *Hassgesang* (translation by Barbara Henderson, as it appeared in the *New York Times* of 15 October 1914), are:

> Hate by water and hate by land,
> Hate of the head and hate of the hand,
> Hate of the hammer and hate of the crown,
> Hate of seventy millions choking down.
> We love as one, we hate as one,
> We have one foe and one alone –
> ENGLAND!

Whilst England was the focus of the propaganda effort, it was over the skies of Belgium that the Zeppelin would first prove itself as a weapon capable of waging war.

---

3. https://withoutliftingafinger.blogspot.com/2012/03/hymn-of-hate-by-ernst-lissauer.html.

Chapter Three

Andenken aus Belgien (Souvenirs from Belgium)

On the night of 6 August 1914 Germany carried out the first air attack on a European city, when Army Zeppelin *ZVI* bombed Liège, killing nine civilians. The Belgian city, known to the Germans as Lüttich, was subject to aerial assault by artillery shells, as there were no such things as specialised Zeppelin bombs in these opening days of the conflict. However, the airship's inadequate lift kept it at low altitude so that bullets and shrapnel from the defending Belgian forces managed to penetrate the gasbags. It limped homewards, but was completely wrecked after having to be set down in a forest near Bonn.

On the night of 24/25 August 1914 Antwerp became the next Belgian city to be bombarded by Zeppelin *ZIX*, with ten people being killed, including women and children. Again, improvised ordnance was employed with 21cm mortar shells, weighing 120kg each being dropped. Each shell had a strip of blanket tied to

Hurrah for our Zeppelin! The raid on Lüttich (Liège) quickly became the subject of patriotic postcards. The image gives the raider the correct designation, *ZVI*. (*Pub. Albert Ebner, Munich*)

Das Eingreifen des Z.VI. im Kampf um Lüttich am 6.Aug.14

A dramatic interpretation of the attack on Liège by noted press illustrator, Felix Schwormstädt. The city commanded the railway crossing over the River Meuse and its valiant defence held up the German advance to the French frontier.

The Bombardment of Antwerp. The gasworks and the cathedral are both in flames and Count Zeppelin, encircled by the victor's laurels, looks on. (*Pub. Franz Josef Huber, Munich*)

Antwerp before its fall. The artist has placed English servicemen and Belgian soldiers in the middle of the civilians fleeing the bombardment. (*Pub. C.C. Meinhold & Soehne, Dresden*)

A dramatic hand–coloured field-sketch of the bombing of Antwerp. (*Pub. Wezei & Naumann, Leipzig*)

Belgium is forced to surrender after 'enjoying' Zeppelin-Pralines. The chocolate-filled bon-bon was created in Brussels in 1912. (*Pub. Hermann Wolff, Berlin*)

Neu!   **Neu!**

Wundertüte

„Zeppelin"

Gefüllt
mit hübschen Überraschungen
und teilweise Bonbons.

Stück 10 Pfennig.

Nachdruck verboten.

=== **Wundertüte** ===
für
10 Pfennig.

Das Lied vom Zeppelin.

Vor Lüttichs Toren mit drohender Macht!
Der Ruf der Geschütze durchdröhnt die Nacht.
Ja unsere Tapfern die haben's gewagt!
Die Feste muß fallen noch ehe es tagt!
Und droben am Himmel ein Wetter braust;
Wie's in den Lüften rattert und saust!
Wer schwebt denn hoch über Zinnen und Turm?
Ein Riesenvogel in Wolken und Sturm:
    Hurra Zeppelin!

Nun kommt von oben mit surrendem Schall
Wohl Bombe auf Bombe mit rasendem Fall,
Die wühlend sich in den Schanzen verrammt!
Es blitzet und kracht, — es zündet und flammt.
Bis drunten die fröhliche Waffentat
Der Deutschen die Feste bezwungen hat.
Da wendet der Vogel den mächtigen Flug,
Als wollte er sagen: für heut' ist's genug!
    Hurra Zeppelin!

Nur Mut und Begeist'rung erfüllt die Armee,
Die furchtlosen Streiter zu Land und zur See,
Die Könige der Lüfte, o tu's ihnen gleich,
Als Schrecken der Feinde beschirmen das Reich!
Flieg hin, flieg hin durch heiligen Krieg,
Vom Höchsten geleitet von Sieg zu Sieg,
Und jauchzen, will's Gott, unsern Helden wir zu,
Dann wollen wir jubeln: „Ein Held bist auch du"
    Hurra Zeppelin!

This seemingly innocent 10 pfennig lucky bag, to be filled with surprises and candies, also carries a patriotic song celebrating the Zeppelin that bombed Liège.

The quote on the postcard is from a Friedrich Schiller poem, *Das Leid von der Glocke* (The Song of the Bell) published in 1799, and translates to: 'That the work may praise the Master, Though the blessing comes from on high'.

one end in an effort to make it fall head on. Belgian authorities reported eight explosions with buildings hit including the royal palace and, because the royal family was in residence at the time, it was claimed that the raid was made with the intent of their assassination.[1] Antwerp had been bypassed by the German armies on their initial advance through Belgium and only fell on 9 October 1914 after a month-long siege.

Zeppelin raids were now a deadly reality and the raids over Belgium seemed more like an act of deliberate terror than a tactical ploy. The names of the bombed and captured Belgian cities, such as Liège, Antwerp, Namur and Brussels became a form of shorthand in the mass-media to underline German successes.

The *Sachsen*, a former DELAG ship hastily refitted for military service by the army at the outbreak of the war, had also bombed Antwerp on the night of 1 September 1914. Peter Strasser, who was destined to become 'Leader of Airships', was taught about airship handling on board the *Sachsen* by Captain Ernst A. Lehmann (later to become the captain of the *Graf Zeppelin* and the ill-fated *Hindenburg*). The *Sachsen*

---

1. There was a similar accusation following the first raid on England on 19 January 1915, as Navy Zeppelin *L4* had passed over the Sandringham Estate shortly before its attack on King's Lynn.

had already carried almost 5,000 commercial passengers in some 200 trips, covering a distance of 13,700 miles.

Count Zeppelin's nephew Baron Max von Gemmingen (1862–1924), was the general staff officer assigned to the *Sachsen* and later in the war he developed, together with Lehmann, the *Spähkorb* or spy/observation car, which could be lowered through the clouds on a steel cable in order to inconspicuously observe the ground and to help navigate the airship.

The *Sachsen* is referenced directly in the humorous postcard on the previous page. As readers will note from many later illustrations, where identification numbers are shown on a Zeppelin, they are almost always simply 'Zeppelin 1' or have an incorrect 'Z' designation.

German postcard publishers were quick to produce images demonstrating the might of this fearsome weapon with numerous cards celebrating the raids on Belgium. A good example is shown below, where the Deutsche Michel is receiving one of the Belgian forts as a souvenir from a soldier, who is handed the Iron Cross in return. Michel is leading the German fleet with an overcrowded basket of troops on his back and there are massed ranks of Zeppelins and aircraft above.

The worried looking Allied soldiers are saying that they have made a mistake in taking on the might of Germany. (*Pub. Hans Schaal, Stuttgart*)

Chapter Four

Mit diesen Rab-Vögeln werden wir schon fertig! (It won't take us long to deal with these birds of prey!)

In addition to the vilification of Allied troops, propaganda also extended to the mockery of the leaders of the countries opposing Germany and the characteristics of the nations themselves, to include those that remained neutral at the outset of the conflict.

In this chapter, two fascinating postcards, which also incorporate the Zeppelin as a major component, are analysed.

Firstly, the image on the next page depicts the leaders of the Allies as rapacious birds of prey with their sharp talons hovering over the German and Austro-Hungarian Empires. Again, 'the Two' are encircled, but they will see off their enemies with the assistance of a Zeppelin armed with a machine gun, which is being fired from an upper platform. It is also dropping a bomb on the blockading warships. The artist, Alfred von Schrötter,[1] helpfully provided a key to identify each of the birds, starting at the bottom left of the 'flock' as follows:

B. Albert I King of the Belgians

F. President Raymond Poincaré of France

R. Tsar Nicholas II of Russia

E. King George V of 'England'

J. Emperor Taishō of Japan. The addition of 'Kiau-Tschau' refers to Tsingtao, the German garrison and naval base in north-west China (now Qingdao in Shandong province) that valiantly held out for several months against an Anglo-Japanese taskforce.

S. Peter I, King of Serbia

M. Nikola (or Nicholas) I, King of Montenegro

Ä. (Ägypten – Egypt) This is likely to be Sultan Hussein Kamel wearing the traditional tarboosh or fez.

---

1. Austrian-born, von Schrötter (1856–1935) is best known as a figure and landscape painter and teacher at the drawing academy at Graz.

The Zeppelin helps to despatch the Allied birds of prey.

The inclusion of Egypt as an addition to the traditional 'Seven' is unusual and was probably included in support of the Ottoman Empire's claims to the Protectorate.

The defenders have also loosened three feathers, Lüttich and Brüssel (Liège and Brussels) and Metz. Metz had been annexed in 1871 and was an important garrison city of the Imperial German Army with its own Zeppelin hangar.

The second postcard (below), the *Humoristische Landkarte* (Humorous Atlas), provides a visual representation of the position in Europe in late 1914, complete with a selection of stirring slogans and caricatures specific to each country. The Allied nations are coloured green, with the Central Powers in red and neutral countries in yellow. Moving around the map clockwise, you will see:

Finland: 'The sun of freedom is rising!' Finland was a Grand Duchy in the Russian Empire and the defeat of Russia will set it free.

Russia: (1) 'Is Hindenburg already through to the rear?' referring, no doubt, to the crushing defeat of the Russian Second Army at the Battle of Tannenberg. (2) 'Rearwards ride the heroes To announce the victory to the Tsar.' The Cossack carries a knout, a Russian whip used to inflict punishment.

The Black Sea is the sphere of operations for the battle cruiser SMS *Göben* and the light cruiser SMS *Breslau*. They were transferred to the Ottoman Empire on

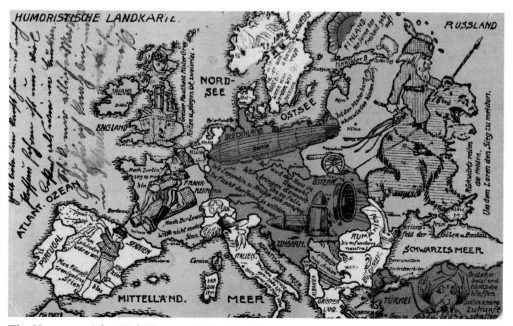

The Humorous Atlas. (*Pub. Hermann Becker, Munich*)

16 August 1914, helping to bring Turkey into the war on the side of the Central Powers and renamed *Yavuz Sultan Selim* and *Midilli* respectively. Turkey had ordered two Dreadnoughts, *Sultan Osman* and *Reshadieh*, from British yards but, before war was declared, these were impounded on the orders of Winston Churchill, even as Turkish crews were carrying out sea trials on one of them. They became Royal Navy ships as *Agincourt* and *Erin*. Entry is also forbidden to the Dardanelles.

Turkey: 'German spirit and Turkish weapons will forge our future.' Sultan Mehmed V is smoking a traditional Turkish water pipe or *nargile*.

Romania and Bulgaria: 'Neutral until further notice.' Romania did not enter the war on the side of the Allies until 27 August 1916. The country sits above a caricature of the Bulgarian King, Ferdinand I. Bulgaria finally declared for the Central Powers on 11 October 1915.

Serbia: 'has to die'. This is a piece of wordplay as an extra 'i' has been placed in *sterben* (to die) to make it rhyme with *Serbien*.

Germany and Austro Hungary: 'If the Russians come in numbers, we will still cut them down. Where Zeppelin and Krupp join forces, then the enemy flees in disarray.' The two powerhouses of military technology were the embodiment of the German Empire.

Italy: 'They taunt us, but we don't care. We're staying neutral.' Prior to the war, Italy had sided with Germany and Austria-Hungary in the Triple Alliance. However, Italy waited until May 1915 before declaring its hand for the Allies.

France: 'I set off for Berlin and ended up in Bordeaux.' This is a direct reference to the relocation of the French government to Bordeaux from Paris by President Poincaré due to the pressure of the German forces in September 1914. As befits a trip to Bordeaux, the stereotypical French officer is riding a wine bottle.

Spain: 'It would really lovely to be here, where they only fight bulls.' Spain clung staunchly to its neutrality and is symbolised here as a bullfighter.

England: 'You're a loud-mouth Mister Grey, Taunting and winning are two different things.'

Foreign Secretary Sir Edward Grey was described as 'a false rascal', 'mad or an idiot', or a 'scoundrel' in Germany. This vitriol had its roots in misunderstandings during the July Crisis of 1914 when the German leaders hoped for British neutrality in a continental war. Their bitter disappointment led to feelings of betrayal, and Grey became a focal point of this resentment.[2]

Sweden: 'We won't allow ourselves to be pulled hither and yon. If anyone attacks us, we will bite them.' Sweden was a prosperous nation with a considerable military and maintained its neutrality, as did its Scandinavian neighbours Denmark and Norway.

2. Mombauer, Annika. 'Sir Edward Grey, Germany, and the Origins of the First World War: A Re-Evaluation.' *The International History Review*, 38 (2) pp.301–25.

Chapter Five

Was Kommt Dort Von der Höh?
(What Comes There from on Yonder?)

I n the autumn of 1914, before the war settled into the daily and brutal grind of trench warfare, the Zeppelin was portrayed as a weapon that could be capable of supporting front-line troops and not just bombing enemy cities. The reality was somewhat different, as the poor handling of Zeppelins on both the Eastern and Western Fronts quickly resulted in losses caused by ground fire.

However, propaganda postcard artists were quick to seize on the image of the Zeppelin over the battlefield as another way of showcasing its superiority over the enemy and used a combination of hatred, ridicule and humour to do so. The

"Hurrah! The Zeppelin carousel, Flies elegantly and fast. The enemy clamours with rage and horror. Oh God, what blessings come from above!" On the base of the carousel are English, French and Russian soldiers. From the Deutsche *Kriegsbilderbogen*, a satarical publication. (*Pub. Bilderbogen-Verlag, Berlin*)

The caption is not an easy one to translate, but I have interpreted it as being the voice of the Frenchmen on the ground saying: 'Please don't drop these things on us. We'll save you the trouble and do it ourselves'.

Was kommt dort von der Höh!

Allied troops under attack from a Zeppelin. The soldier with the dagger in his belt is probably Serbian. (*Pub. Schaar & Dathe, Trier*)

Aerial Greetings from Berlin! The Eastern Front is the scene of a savage assault on the Russian army with scatological overtones. (*Pub. K. V. Berlin*)

Zeppelin was a proven symbol of modern warfare in the eyes of the German public, and having one (or more) on its postcards would also, no doubt, help to increase a publisher's sales and some excellent examples are highlighted in this chapter.

Postmarked 13 November 1914 and sent from a military hospital in Hamburg, the image on page 35 shows Count Zeppelin in his typical 'Onkel' (Uncle) Zeppelin attire, wearing a small-brimmed captain's hat and short jacket. He is astride a Zeppelin dropping bombs from his picnic basket on the French soldiers below. He is leading a fleet of Zeppelins and aircraft. The Zeppelin itself is representative of the pre-war type with its horizontal stabilizers.

'Was Kommt Dort Von der Höh?' is a jovial German student song sung to receive the first-year students. The new students, called foxes because of their wariness and apprehension, are led to the waiting group of students by the Foxmajor, a senior-class man who acts as guide for the freshmen. Here, opposite, the song is parodied as the Allied troops are on the receiving end of a bomb dropped from 'on yonder'.[1]

Destructive airpower is also shown for comic effect in the remarkable postcard above. The Cossacks and their horses are literally blown to pieces as they receive

---

1. http://www.traditioninaction.org/Cultural/Music_P_files/P038_Fox.htm.

aerial greetings from Berlin. The translated rhyme does not make a huge amount of sense at first glance.

> What's that down there, more Cossacks?
> We'll pour cocoa on their hats
> And throw dumplings at their stomachs
> For target practice

However, the consensus is that it is a piece of none too subtle toilet humour with the copywriter using 'Kakao' (to pour the cocoa) and 'schiessen' (to shoot the targets) as euphemisms for what he really wanted to say, being 'kacken' (to shit) and 'scheissen' (also, unsurprisingly, to shit). So, essentially, the Zeppelin's bombs have defecated on the Cossacks and the dumplings (also bombs) have caused the Cossacks to fill their trousers.

The Russian bear is at the centre of the image below where a fleet of Zeppelins drop bombs on the sorry looking creature with a bloodied nose and moulting fur. The bear is carrying its fellow Allies on its back and the French cockerel has lost its feathers. What looks to be a dishevelled English gent with a top hat and high collar

'The Good Companions' is a brutal characterisation of the blooded and beaten Allies under the relentless assault of the Zeppelin fleet. (*Pub. S. & G. Saulsohn, Berlin*)

clings grimly to the bear's fur. It is likely that the postcard was published shortly after the victorious Battle of Tannenberg.

The German fleet is also shown in the background, adding to the carnage, and if you look closely at the bear and its passengers, they are covered in lice. Does this simply emphasise the poor state of the Allied forces or does it also employ the German idiom to put 'a louse in the fur' (*'laus in pelz'*)? This means someone who later turns out to be harmful and, perhaps, the lice represent the Triple Entente and its 'behind closed doors' diplomacy.

In a much more dignified manner, a Zeppelin could even transport prisoners of war in the mind of an artist looking to rally public morale. A victorious Zeppelin is shown returning to Berlin with its haul of Allied prisoners in the image below, including bandaged Cossacks and bewildered Frenchmen (some without boots), who are joined by their colonial troops. There is also a contingent of English *'kilts-truppen'*. The Zeppelin itself is looking a little battle-scarred, but has been triumphant despite the odds.

Finally, it was not only artistic or photo-montaged images of Zeppelins and cartoons of harassed Allied troops that were used to capture the mood of the public. The photographic studio was used with some effect, with photographer's models portraying troops of all combatants.

'The quickest way to reach Berlin. Fly high you mighty Zeppelin.' (*Pub. Ottmar Zieher, Munich*)

The Fear of 'Made in Germany' has never been so great. English "Kilt-troops" flee from German technology.

Our Zeppelins have been a riotous success. A wide variety of allied troops suffer at the hands of Zeppelin 'No. 168'. (*Pub. Wilhelm S. Schröder Nachf., Berlin*)

Nicht alles Gute kommt von oben.

'Not everything good comes from above.' Subverting James 1:17, the Zeppelin is not the divine presence that the Allied troops are praying for. (*Pub. E.A. Schwerdtfeger & Co, Berlin*)

The use of backdrops and props incorporating a Zeppelin or an aircraft were used by pre-war portrait photographers. This was popular with groups of soldiers who would have been in training as part of their short-service conscription and a group photograph as a memento, or as something to be given to families back home, would have been a part of their shared experience. This trend continued once war was declared. Photo paper with pre-printed postcard backs was the most widely available at this time, so customers usually received their studio portraits in this format, whether they intended to post them or not.

Posing for the camera, these four fine chaps are part of a photo-montage, complete with a Zeppelin, prepared by a local photographic studio. The phrase on the Aviatik's wing translates as 'Woe to you England'.

Chapter Six

England wird abgebrannt
(England shall be destroyed by fire)

Zeppelin, flieg!
Hilf uns im krieg,
Flieg nach England,
England wird abgebrannt,
Zeppelin, flieg!

'Fly, Zeppelin! Help us in the war. Fly to England, England shall be destroyed by fire. Zeppelin, fly!' Such was the hymn which the children sang; such the refrain which greeted the aged inventor wherever he went.[1]

This chilling variation of the German children's rhyme '*Maikäfer*' (cockchafer – a beetle), similar to the English 'Ladybird, Ladybird', became popular as the clamour for the Zeppelin to raid the home of its enemy grew during 1914 and found its way onto a popular postcard (see opposite top). The verse actually dates back to the Thirty Years' War in the first half of the seventeenth century, in which Pomerania was pillaged and suffered heavily.

The use of children, their games and their rhymes, for propaganda purposes was employed by postcard publishers on all sides during the war. Children are presented as imaginary actors in a war that is taking place far away, which they are keen to recreate. Young boys are shown as soldiers and young girls are shown in maternal roles, such as nurses, and this also contributed to the expectation that children would grow up to defend their country. More immediately, it increased the pressure on children to be patriotic and actively support the war effort.

Excellent examples of postcards, which incorporate the Zeppelin, are shown in the images opposite. In the bottom image, the title of which translates as 'How our little ones imagine the air war!', a table and chair, together with other household items, have become an impromptu Zeppelin to bomb a town. The phrase '*Nur ein Viertelstündchen*' used in this postcard literally means 'Only quarter of an hour' and

---

1. Morison, *War on Great Cities – A Study of the Facts*, p. 26.

Count Zeppelin gently releases his 'Maikäfer' towards England on a mission of destruction.

'Little Air War' by Austrian painter and illustrator Pauli Ebner (1873–1949), best known for her drawings of small girls. (*Pub. M Munk, Vien*)

Children enact a Zeppelin raid on London. (*Pub. Carl Andelfinger & Cie., Munich*)

is a recurrent German motif. In this instance, its use is similar to 'It will all be over by Christmas', as the children believe that the war will not last for long.

Above, is a postcard by the artist P.O.E., who is best known for his depictions of patriotic children.[2] Here the children are pretending to be frightened Londoners and Count Zeppelin is, again, portrayed in his 'Onkel' persona. There is one child on a chamber pot and the British fleet of paper boats is also blockaded.

A variety of other imagery was used to reinforce the impression that the Zeppelin was an integral part of Germany's arsenal as well as being a part of its culture. In the bottom image on page 49, being a postcard reproduced from the German satirical magazine *Lustigen Blätter*, Count Zeppelin is cast in the role of the *Klabautermann*, a water kobold (a sprite stemming from Germanic folklore) that assists sailors and fishermen on the Baltic and North Seas in their duties. One omen associated with the *Klabautermann* is that no member of a ship blessed by his presence shall ever set eyes on him. He only ever becomes visible to the crew of a doomed ship and here the Count's appearance seals the fate of the enemy.

In Germany the threat posed by the Royal Navy was of great concern following the pre-war naval arms race and the blockade of the country with the aim of

2. Paul Otto Engelhard, known as P.O.E. (1872–1924) worked as a graphic designer for the War Office in Berlin.

'Where are you going?' ponders this French boy soldier. The Zeppelin heads to England through a starlight sky. (*Pub. Arthur Rehn & Co., Berlin*)

Perhaps the same Zeppelin arrives 'High in the Air', as it is the turn of the English boy soldier to flee.
(*Pub. S. & G. Saulsohn, Berlin*)

Who wants to go to England? A silhouette postcard by Martha Ebeling. Unusually, the Zeppelin is depicted as a giant crocodile. (*Published by the Sekretariat sozialer Studentenarbeit, München-Gladbach*)

Count Zeppelin and his invention take their place in a modern twist on German folklore. (*Pub. Hermann Bergmann, Berlin*)

A postcard which rages against Allied press coverage. (*Pub. Herman Wolff, Berlin*)

starving it into submission. As discussed in Chapter Nine, the Zeppelin played a prominent role in defending German shores and countering the blockade.

Turning to the propaganda war itself, the image above is an interesting postcard as the Zeppelin is being used to drive out the Allies who have been spreading (or spitting) lies about Germany's war effort, with the foreign press being described as 'lie factories' in the discarded newspapers.

The famous London-based Reuters news agency, which was founded in 1851 by Julius Reuter, a German who adopted British nationality, was the subject of particular disdain in Germany. The agency was considered as a propaganda service for the British and was depicted in German propaganda as the 'Lying Toad'.

The caption can be translated as 'The Zeppelin'.

> 'You spit nought but lies into the world! (Referring to the Foreign press)
> I spit on you, you lying brood,
> and teach you to run.'

In contrast, the *Wolffsche Telegraphenbüro* (Wolff Telegraphic Bureau), established in 1871, was the central source for news in Germany during the war and was singled out for derision in French and Italian propaganda postcards.

Chapter Seven

Dass ganz Paris sich in die Hosen macht!
(And all of Paris fills its pants!)

W hilst the devastation of London was seen as the ultimate prize, it was believed that Zeppelins would also be used to raid Paris due, in part, to the proximity of German airship bases established in Belgium. Both London and Paris were nerve centres of their countries and surrounded by vast rings of factories engaged in war work and were, therefore, viable targets.

However, there were significantly fewer raids on the French capital, although there were soon sufficient numbers of Zeppelins to justify simultaneous attacks. In reality Paris was well defended with in excess of 200 guns and only suffered lightly in comparison to the concentrated raids on London that took place in 1915 and 1916 and was praised for the efficiency and vigour of her defence.

There were just three occasions when Paris was attacked by army airships, namely on 21 March 1915 and on 29 and 30 January 1916. The first of the January 1916

The Great Race to Paris 1914. (*Pub. Brüder Kohn, Wien*)

Zeppelin auf einer Spritztour
nach Paris – London.

A gargantuan Count Zeppelin is on his way from Paris to London ready to literally 'sprinkle' the Allied capitals with bombs. Note the fleeing troops below. (*Pub. Arthur Albrecht & Cie, Karlsruhe*)

·Zeppeline· Nachtfahrt·nach· England·über· M... ·in·Flandern· 28.Ⅱ.15.

An evocative image of Zeppelins heading across the Flanders battlefield to England, possibly sketched by a German soldier. 'M' could stand for Maubeuge, which was used as a base for Zeppelin raids. (*Pub. Xaver Rief, Regensburg*)

raids was the most effective, with explosive bombs killing twenty-four people and injuring thirty-two. There were, however, numerous aeroplane raids on Paris and its suburbs, beginning with a lone Taube attack on 30 August 1914. On the night of 30 January 1918, Gotha bombers carried out the first of many raids. Aircraft inflicted 804 casualties, the vast majority occurring in the first quarter of 1918.[1]

In 1917 the idea of building a replica of Paris was considered as a way to fool the German bombers into dropping their destructive loads outside of the city. Parts of the decoy city were built, including a fake running train and some factory buildings, but the end of the war came before the project could be completed and it was quickly dismantled.

Paris was also subjected to a form of attack which London was fortunate to escape, being the long-range bombardment in 1918 by colossal siege guns. This indiscriminate form of attack from a distance of some seventy-five miles resulted in more persons being killed in Paris itself during forty-four days' bombardment from

---

1. Morison, op. cit., p.175.

Serie 63/4 Weftl. Kriegsſchaupl: Ein Zeppelin
wirft zum erſten male Bomben auf Paris

A dramatic rendering of the first Zeppelin raid on Paris. (*Pub Josef Eberle, Vien*)

'The daily air raid on Paris. Not only does it spread panic by dropping bombs, it also delivers news of German victories to the city'. Captions on streamers: Antwerp has been occupied – You are next in line. Antwerp has fallen – You're next. (*Pub. Wilhelm S. Schröder Nachf., Berlin*)

March to August 1918 than the combined efforts of Zeppelins and aircraft during the previous three and a half years.

For propaganda purposes, German postcard artists had a fascination with the aerial bombardment of Paris. The city's landmarks, such as the iconic Eiffel Tower, were easy shorthand to demonstrate the superiority of German technology over the French. However, in order to reach Paris from its bases, Zeppelins would have to make overland voyages and, therefore, be liable to detection either by sight or sound all of the way.

Amongst the postcards used to illustrate this chapter, the images overleaf are striking in that they again reflect the German obsession with toilet humour. As military historian Cyril Falls remarked, 'We must recall that the latrine has always had a fascination for the German soldier, and that during the War one used to find on postcards in prisoner's pockets pictures of this necessity of nature in use.'

On page 57, a futuristic looking Zeppelin is seen bombing the Place de la République with the translated caption reading:

> The Zeppelin drops its bombs from a height
> And the Parisians fill their pants with shite

'Oh my God, the puffs and rants. All of Paris fills its pants!' French soldiers are in various states of distress in the shadow of the Eiffel Tower.

The pants of General Galliéni and many of his staff fill up in fear of the Zeppelin. Others pray or vomit! (*Pub. Hermann Wolff, Berlin*)

The central figure in the postcard is General Joseph Simon Galliéni (1849–1916), who was appointed Military Governor of Paris in August 1914. He immediately set to work on improving the fortifications of the capital and is famous for rushing reinforcements to the Sixth Army in a fleet of taxicabs during the First Battle of the Marne.

It should be noted, in passing, that French postcard publishers, like their British counterparts, also produced morale-boosting postcards, ridiculing the ineffectiveness of the Zeppelin raids. The Kaiser and Count Zeppelin were singled out for mockery by the French, whilst the crews were described as thieves, pirates and assassins (overleaf).

Whilst Paris received cursory attention from Zeppelins, there was only one target that mattered to the German public: London.

German artists saw Count Zeppelin as most respectable, but their French counterparts leaned to the sinister. (*Pub E. Le Deley, Paris*)

Chapter Eight

Zeppelin über London

London was the vital spot, the 'solar plexus' of the nation … . With London brought low, as the German people fondly hoped would be the case, through the agency of their incomparable flying services, England could be made to sue for peace.

Air Commodore L.E.O. Charlton.[1]

Incited by Lissauer's 'Hymn of Hate' and buoyed by the successes over Belgium, the German public clamoured for Zeppelins to bring terror and panic to the streets of London. England could be destroyed with fire and, once the army and navy had sufficient numbers available following delivery of the new P-class Zeppelin, the High Command honed its plans to strike.

Kaiser Wilhelm finally permitted the bombing of London in May 1915 but targets were to be restricted to areas east of the Tower of London. Whilst these restrictions would be lifted in July, the Kaiser's lofty ideals not to touch historic buildings and royal palaces were admirable but misguided. The crude bombsights and haphazard navigational tools did not permit such pinpoint accuracy. However, the river Thames was an unmistakable marker on any cloudless night, despite the lighting restrictions and other counter-measures put in place.

The evening of 31 May 1915 marked the bombing of London for the first time by Army Zeppelin *LZ38*, commanded by Hauptmann Erich Linnarz. This was the first of the P-Class to enter service and Linnarz had already given his crew the necessary experience with a number of successful raids on the east of England, including Bury St Edmunds, Ramsgate and Southend-on-Sea, over the preceding month.

There were forty-two casualties with seven killed and thirty-five injured, as the threat of a large-scale attack on London had been brought to deadly fruition. Linnarz became a popular hero and the raid also satisfied the German public's

---

1. Charlton, *War Over England*, pp.16–17. Air Commodore Lionel Evelyn Oswald Charlton (1879–1958) was one of the most prominent prophets of aerial Armageddon in 1930s Britain.

East of the Tower of London was the Kaiser's line of demarcation for the first Zeppelin attack on London in May 1915. (*Pub. Wezel & Naumann AG, Leipzig*)

growing demand for retaliation against Britain's attempt to starve out Germany through its naval blockade.

As the nights got longer, any respite that Londoners enjoyed after Linnarz's initial raid came to an end. From early August to mid-October 1915, Zeppelin raids persisted as these now more powerful and better-designed airships could reach London easily from the remote naval airship stations in northern Germany, rather than from the army bases in Belgium, which were found to be vulnerable to attack. There were four successful raids on London in this period, with the raid of 8/9 September 1915 by Navy Zeppelin *L13* being, in material terms, the most destructive raid of the entire war, with damage valued at £530,787. The Zeppelin was commanded by Heinrich Mathy, known and feared as the most daring and audacious of all the raiders.

The subsequent raid on the night of 13/14 October 1915, which became known as the 'Theatreland' raid, claimed forty-seven lives and left 102 people injured. *L15*, commanded by Joachim Breithaupt, led the assault with a ten-minute west-to-east bombing run across the heart of the capital from the Strand to Whitechapel.

Even before Linnarz's initial success, German postcard publishers had already begun to produce images of London under attack (see the example on page 62, which is postmarked 19 March 1915). Back in Germany, reports of successful raids,

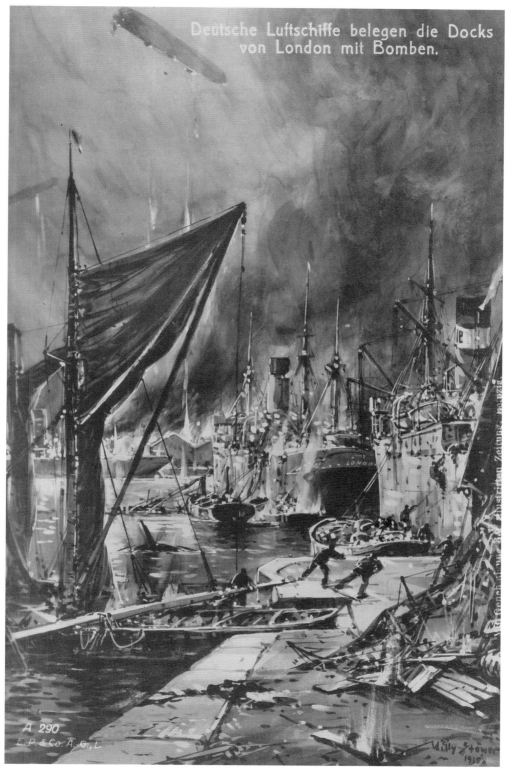

London's Docks are bombed in this dramatic Willy Stöwer illustration. (*Pub. E. P. & Co. A.G.L., Leipzig*)

The caption on the reverse of this postcard explains that the airship bombing London has been shot at by a local anti-aircraft battery, which protects valuable buildings from shelling. Pure propaganda, as the postcard was sent almost three months before the first London raid! (*Pub. Hans Schinzinger, Hohenheim*)

Den Manen Eduard's
das eingekreiste Deutschland.

Das eingekreiste London.

'To the spectre of Edward VII, who encircled Germany, (we now present) Encircled London!' Big Ben fell silent in October 1914 and did not toll again until November 1916. A charity postcard for the Saxony Red Cross. (*Pub. C.C. Meinhold & Söhne, Dresden*)

Das Schwert des Damokles.

The Sword of Damocles hangs over John Bull, cowering inside the Tower of London. From the series produced for the satirical magazine *Kladderadatsch* (onomatopoeic for 'Crash'). (*Pub. Gerh Stalling, Oldenburg*)

ZEPPELIN über LONDON.

Zeppelin over St Paul's Cathedral. It is reminiscent of 'St Paul's Survives', the iconic Blitz photograph taken by Herbert Mason in the early hours of 30 December 1940.

Zeppelin Kommt! Panic in London, as citizens of all classes shove their way into an underground station to seek refuge in the shadow of Tower Bridge.

Zeppelin kommt!

This time the Houses of Parliament provide the backdrop to a scene of chaos. (*Both postcards — Pub. Gebrüder Dietrich, Leipzig*)

which were often taken from inaccurate reports made by the airships' commanders, were exaggerated for propaganda purposes. Stylised versions of these events usually took the form of an artist's impression or a photograph of a Zeppelin superimposed above a stock picture of London landmarks, such as the Tower of London, Tower Bridge, St Paul's Cathedral or the Houses of Parliament. Ironically, these were the historic buildings that the Kaiser had originally sought to protect.

There were also striking cards produced by one of the best postcard artists, Arthur Thiele.[2] In the images on pages 66 and 67, he parodies his popular pre-war 'Zeppelin Kommt' postcards (see the image on page 3), in which he portrayed delighted citizens rushing to see the Zeppelin approaching their town, but now the tone was much darker. The back of each card includes a patriotic song of encouragement to terrorise London based on Thiele's artwork. The scene depicted in the image on page 66 has its basis in fact as, from the time of the earliest attacks, it was the custom for underground stations to offer shelter to people caught in the streets during a raid. The song translates as follows:

> *Zeppelin visit to London*
> Comes a Zeppelin a–flying,
> Arrow-straight across the sea,
> Over London, proudly floating,
> Flying high and threateningly
> With terrified looks upon their faces,
> Crying out from far around,
> All flee Tower Bridge's open spaces,
> For refuge in the Underground

---

2. Carl Robert Arthur Thiele (born 2 November 1860 in Leipzig, died 18 June 1936 in the same city) was largely known outside Germany for his postcards of anthropomorphic animals, especially dachshunds and cats.

Chapter Nine

Der Beherrscher der Meere
(The Ruler of the Seas)

Whilst the German public demanded that the destructive power of the Zeppelin should be unleashed, this was only a small part of its role during the war. Their most dramatic feats were undoubtedly the raids on England, but the rapid improvement in home defence eventually made this too dangerous a proposition.

A more mundane role was the Zeppelin's support of naval operations, undertaking the valuable task of fleet reconnaissance with the Imperial German Navy in the North Sea and the Baltic. Captain Ernst Lehmann summarised the work of the wartime airships, noting that seventy-two airships, among them sixty-two Navy

A Zeppelin supports an imagined seaborne invasion of England by the Marines. The rhyme includes the stirring refrain 'We are Blue, we are a storm that firm will stand, We are the first ones over to the other land.'

Prof. M. Zeno Diemer, Zeppelin über der Schlachtflotte

Artist Michael Zeno Diemer provides a fine example of a Zeppelin co-operating with the battle fleet. (*Pub. Vereinigung der Kunstfreunde, Berlin-Schöneberg*)

Freudige Begegnung

A joyful encounter between a Zeppelin and U-boat. (*Pub. Wilhelm S. Schröder Nachf., Berlin*)

Zeppelins, made a total of 1,148 long distance patrol flights.[1] In this task, the Zeppelin thoroughly justified itself for only a fraction of the energy and cost, in material and human terms, that it expended in raiding England.

In view of the limited numbers of operational craft, Zeppelins were cautiously used at first to provide a defensive shield around the navy, as opposed to undertaking long-distance strategic scouting. However, it was soon recognised that the long endurance of airships provided an uninterrupted aerial platform and a third dimension to naval operations, lengthening the range of view to unprecedented distances.

Many images of Zeppelins over the fleet were produced, as this was a further reminder of the versatility of the iconic airship. German postcard publishers had a rich tradition of nautical illustrators to draw upon. This included Willy Stöwer, who was said to be the Kaiser's favourite naval painter, Michael Zeno Diemer[2] and Hans Rudolf Schulze. Artists of this calibre were also quick to incorporate and accurately reproduce Zeppelins and aeroplanes into their work, which were reproduced as popular postcards.

---

1. Lehmann & Mingos, *The Zeppelins*, p.163
2. Michael Zeno Diemer (1867–1939); his son, Franz (1889–1954) joined Dornier in Friedrichshafen, the home of the Zeppelin, as test pilot in July 1921.

John Bull in Angsten

Mit Zeppelin und U —
Jagt man mich immerzu
Zu aller Hohn und Spotte! —
Ich bin in größten Nöten,
Mein Anseh'n ging schon flöten
Durch diese Luxusflotte!

John Bull with the 'wind up' as he is hunted high and low by the 'luxury-fleet' of Zeppelins and U-boats. (*Pub. Emil Bürckner, Leipzig*)

By June 1915 the Naval Airship Division had been elevated to a permanent arm of the fleet and the building of additional airships and sheds was prioritised. The Zeppelin's air reconnaissance abilities enabled it to undertake a variety of tasks, such as combating enemy submarines, protecting minesweeping flotillas from surprise attack and locating and marking minefields, so that the flotillas could carry out their work. Zeppelins could also be used to co-operate tactically with both the fleet and submarines and report the movements of enemy commercial vessels.

To counteract the Allied naval blockade, which cut off approximately one-third of Germany's importation of foodstuffs, Germany imposed its own blockade of British ports through the declaration of unrestricted submarine warfare in February 1915. The tactic was abandoned on 1 September 1915, following the loss of American lives in the torpedoed liners RMS *Lusitania* and SS *Arabic*, and was not resumed until 1 February 1917.

German postcard artists seized on the success of the twin threats of Zeppelins and submarines against England and, in another Arthur Thiele design on the previous page (postmarked 31 December 1915), a grotesque John Bull has 'got the wind up', as England is harried by a 'Luxury Fleet' of Zeppelins and U-boats.

'Goddam, that's a fine soup I've landed myself in!' John Bull faces the consequences of challenging the might of Germany. The vessel approaching London is the SS *Königin Luise*, the first German naval loss of the war on 5 August 1914. Its inclusion acknowledges the bravery of her crew. (*Pub. Sächsische Verlagsanstalt, Dresden*)

The English disease. An English soldier represents the beleaguered navy. Note the patched umbrella. (*Pub.Wm. Baron, Berlin*)

HM Old England 'Gentlemen, take cover quickly, the Zeppelin is upon us.' The postcard plays on the stereotype of all Englishmen carrying umbrellas.

Britannia is, demonstrably, not ruling the waves as German sea power sees through the Admiralty's order that British ships should fly neutral flags in the war zone to deceive German submarines.

Whilst unrestricted submarine warfare was directed against enemy ships, it also applied to ships flying neutral flags, given the suspicion that these were being misused by enemy ships. This is graphically illustrated in the image opposite, where a corpulent John Bull desperately reaches out to the flag-bearing neutral nations, including the USA, for assistance as he is being dragged beneath the waves by submariners, depicted as mermen. The Zeppelin flies overhead, proudly displaying the *Reichkriegsflagge*.

Staying with the scatological theme explored in earlier chapters, the English sailors are 'occupied' in their ports, below, by the commanding presence of a Zeppelin and unable, therefore, to get off their chamber pots. This was a commonly used theme to demonstrate that the Royal Navy was too frightened to engage in a decisive battle. 'Occupied' toilets were also used in propaganda to represent occupied Belgian territory and, opposite, the English soldiers are unable to relieve themselves in Ostend under attack from a Zeppelin with the inevitable result.

In May 1916, at the Battle of Jutland, Zeppelins supported the fleet's advance along the Danish coast, but weather prevented them from taking any part in the action during the day. With clearing weather they did observe some of the muddled night action, but again without effect. However, after the battle, Admiral Reinhard

Occupied! – The result of the Zeppelin's laxative effect. (*Pub. J. Hospe, Staffelstein*)

'Ostende: English beach party here today!' The British were in Ostend in 1914, but were squeezed down the coast to the Yser in the Race to the Sea. (*Pub. Karl Braun, Berlin*)

Scheer, commander of the High Seas Fleet, professed to be pleased with the results of the airship scouting. In August 1916 a timely Zeppelin report saved Scheer from an encounter with the Grand Fleet off Sunderland, which could well have proved disastrous.

Chapter Ten

Treu bis in den Tod (Faithful unto Death): The King Stephen Incident

O ne particular incident involving a downed Zeppelin was seized on by the Germans as further evidence of British atrocities and, therefore, ripe to be exploited as propaganda.

It was the night of a nine-airship raid on the Midlands on 31 January/1 February 1916 and one of the raiders was *L19*, commanded by Kapitänleutnant Odo Loewe. The Navy Zeppelin circled Birmingham and then passed out to sea over Great Yarmouth at 6.30 am, the last raider to leave.

Engine trouble developed soon after and *L19* drifted over the Dutch islands at a low height and was hit repeatedly by rifle fire until it drifted out to sea, driven by a rising south wind. The next morning, the floating wreck of the airship was discovered by a British steam fishing trawler, the *King Stephen*, with William Martin

Faithful unto Death. The North Sea is about to take the life of *L19*'s brave commander. (*Pub. M. L. Carstens, Hamburg*)

Kapitänleutnant Otto Loewe, commander of *L19*. (*Pub. Neue Photographische Gesellschaft, Berlin*)

Skipper Martin's dramatic refusal became worldwide news and divided opinion. (*Pub. Neurdein et Cie, Paris*)

King Stephen, you are damned. The crew hurl insults at the departing trawler. (*Pub. EMM – poss. Emil Mayer, Munich*)

"King Stephen" aber, du bist verflucht

as its skipper and a crew of nine. A group of men were assembled in a makeshift refuge on top of *L19*'s envelope, which towered above the trawler's masts.

Martin refused to rescue *L19*'s crew, which he believed to number twenty, and sailed away, leaving them to their fate. In a later newspaper interview, Martin stated that his crew were unarmed and badly outnumbered, and would have had little chance of resisting the German airmen had they hijacked his vessel and sailed it to Germany. As the trawler left, some of the Germans, it is claimed, shouted out 'Gott strafe England' and shook their fists. It was Martin's intention of finding and alerting a British patrol, but he reached home without sighting another vessel. The crippled airship sank in the black, icy water and all hands perished with her.

The incident received worldwide publicity and divided public opinion. Numerous dramatic postcards were published in Germany, quickly seizing on the growing condemnation of Martin and his crew for leaving the German airmen to die. In Britain, the Bishop of London, Dr Arthur Foley Winnington-Ingram, praised Martin's action for placing the safety of his crew first and not trusting the promises of the Germans. *Flight* magazine of 10 February 1916 was also unequivocal in its support:

> The non-rescue of the crew of this wrecked airship is a direct outcome, and a very stringent object-lesson, of the estimate in which the word of the Germans is now held by civilised people … but from past experience the word of the Hun is now synonymous of nothing less than fraud and lying.[1]

The crew and the Bishop were vilified in the German press, which is reflected in the stark postcard on page 84. The heading reads 'England expects every murderer to do his duty' (The Modern Revised Nelson). The Bishop is addressing the 'heroic crews', depicted as armed and brutish figures, of the *Baralong* and the *King Stephen*. The quote paraphrases the Bishop's speech: 'England is behind you – the chivalry of war has been killed by the Germans.'

HMS *Baralong*, which had been converted from a tramp steamer to became an armed decoy vessel known as a Q ship, had also gained the world's attention through its dramatic and controversial engagement with U-boat *U-27* on 19 August 1915. *Baralong* had sunk the submarine, which was itself about to sink a nearby merchant ship, the *Nicosian*. Some of the German submariners had sought refuge aboard the now abandoned merchantman but the *Baralong*'s commander sent marines aboard to despatch the remaining survivors.

---

1. *Flight* magazine, 10 February 1916, p.111.

2103 O   ROTARY PHOTO, E.C.
THE RT. HON. & RT. REV ARTHUR FOLEY WINNINGTON-INGRAM, D.D.
BISHOP OF LONDON

The controversial Bishop of London who, according to the Frankfurter Zeitung, 'acted less as an apostle of Christian charity than as a jingoistic hate monger.' (*Pub. Rotary Photo, London*)

„ENGLAND ERWARTET, DASS JEDER MORDGESELLE
SEINE PFLICHT TUT".
⟨Der moderne revidierte Nelson⟩

DER BISCHOF VON LONDON zu den „Heldenbesatzungen" des „Baralong" und des „King Stephen": „England steht geschlossen hinter euch! Die Deutschen haben in diesem Kriege alle Ritterlichkeit getötet."   *(Aus der Rede des Bischofs in Stoke Newington.)*

The crews of the *King Stephen* and *Baralong* receive the Bishop of London's sermon.

Karl Goetz Medal commemorating the loss of *L19*. The inscription translates as 'Cursed be the Britons at sea, Cursed their bad conscience; shipwrecked people seeking help were left to sink'.

An England. In Erinnerung an die Mordtaten des „Baralong".

'To England. In memory of the murders of the Baralong'. (*Pub. EMM – poss. Emil Mayer, Munich*)

When he died on 24 February 1917, aged 45, William Martin was said to have been plagued by hate mail and obsessed with the idea that the Germans were tracking him down. His great-grandson believes he may have been mentally damaged by his decision not to help the German crew. 'He was a broken man and he drank heavily. We would call it Post Traumatic Stress Disorder now. I think that's what happened to him.'[2]

---

2. 'Trawlerman's anguished and fateful decision revisited', *Yorkshire Post*, 2 June 2014.

Chapter Eleven

Die neuen Götter der Luft
(The New Gods of the Air)

In the early hours of 3 September 1916, Lieutenant William Leefe Robinson emptied his third drum of ammunition into the body of wooden-framed Schütte-Lanz airship *SL11* from his upward-firing Lewis gun. Londoners had been woken by a crescendo of noise from the anti-aircraft guns and tumbled from their beds to watch the combat unfold above them. They cheered wildly as the army airship caught fire, falling in a roaring mass of flame. It struck the ground at Cuffley, a small Hertfordshire hamlet on the outskirts of the capital.

The new Brock and Pomeroy incendiary ammunition used by Robinson had just shot down the first airship over mainland Britain. As the flaming dirigible fell, illuminating the countryside, Zeppelins of the Naval Airship Division also taking part in the raid were feeling their way across the South East and witnessed this tragedy. They also probably sensed the 'blinding finality that would consume them all'.[1] Robinson's success was swiftly followed by the destruction of three of the newest R-class 'super' Zeppelins over the following weeks through a combination of aircraft armed with the latest ammunition and greatly improved defensive measures.

The German public had been encouraged to place their faith in the power of the Zeppelin and reports of raids were enthusiastically incorporated into postcards and other propaganda. However, the campaign failed to weaken the resolve of the British people to fight and the raids, conversely, had the opposite effect. Whilst there were further sporadic raids into 1917 and 1918, the initiative passed from airships to huge, multi-engine bomber aircraft.

Unrestricted submarine warfare resumed on 1 February 1917 and a new propaganda campaign took place to rationalise this fateful decision by the German High Command, which precipitated America's entry into the war. Thanks to the efforts of the German propaganda machine, the public had also discovered Manfred

---

1. Whitehouse, *The Zeppelin Fighters*, p. 148. The Army Airship Service never raided Britain again and was disbanded within a year.

A SOUVENIR
of the destruction of Zeppelin L.21, by
Lieut. W. L. Robinson V.C. at Cuffle

William Leefe Robinson. The Royal Flying Corps pilot received the fastest Victoria Cross ever rewarded, just 48 hours after he successfully shot down *SL11*. (*Pub. Irvine Series, London*)

A sombre postcard from 1918, as the Deutsche Michel careful conveys a Gotha bomber towards London. (*Pub. H Hohmann, Darmstadt*)

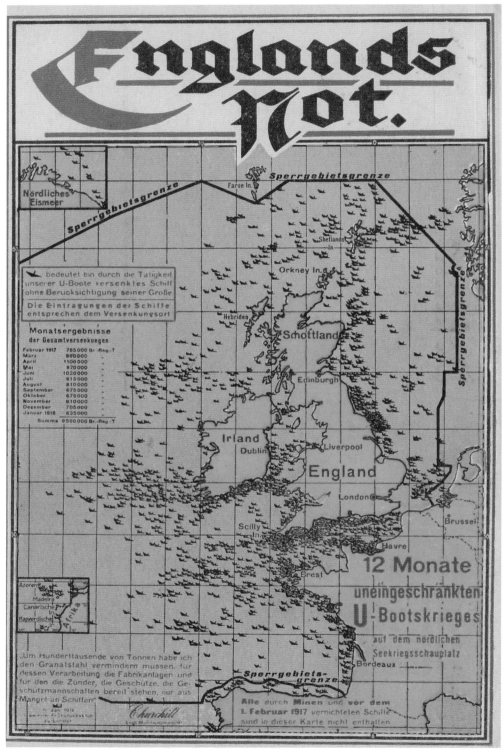

This postcard shows sinkings by U-boats from February 1917 to January 1918. It confirms British records that the worst-ever month was April 1917.

W. Sanke postcard showing the star performers of Jasta 11 taken at Roucourt, with Manfred von Richthofen front and centre. This photograph was taken in the middle of 'Bloody April' 1917, where heavy losses were inflicted on the Royal Flying Corps during the Battle of Arras. The men pictured accounted for 83 enemy aircraft in that month alone.

von Richthofen and his flying circus, and shifted its attention to these new gods of the air. The exploits of these heroes could easily be served up to a war-weary public, as with a few exceptions, it had been the Zeppelin itself, rather than its nameless crews, that had been celebrated.

To offset the psychological effect of airship losses, it was the turn of the U-boat and the fighter pilot to receive the public's acclaim. Peter Strasser's death in August 1918, on what turned out to be the final Zeppelin bombing mission on England, barely attracted attention, although his demise was mourned by the airship crews. Freiherr Treusch von Buttlar Brandenfels, a respected Zeppelin commander, noted the grief that the crews felt and that there was no longer the same interest in flying 'for the spark which Peter had kindled in our breasts had been extinguished'.[2]

By the time of his death on 8 March 1917, the 78-year-old Count Zeppelin was focusing on aircraft design. He had travelled to Berlin to attend an aeronautical exhibition in February 1917 but developed appendicitis and was operated on successfully. However, he developed pneumonia and died. The Count was given a

---

2. von Buttlar-Brandenfels, *Zeppelins Over England*, p.15.

Fregattenkapitän
Strasser

567
Postkartenvertrieb W.Sanke
BERLIN N.37.
Nachdruck wird gerichtlich verfolgt.

Peter Strasser had an unswerving belief in the superiority of the Zeppelin as a weapon of war.
(*Pub. W. Sanke, Berlin*)

FUNERAL OF COUNT ZEPPELIN AT STUTTGART, MARCH 12, 1917.
The King of Wurtemberg is prominent behind the coffin.

A magazine clipping of Count Zeppelin's funeral. His tombstone bears the words of Jesus: 'Dein Glaube hat dir geholfen' ('Your faith has saved you').

state funeral in Stuttgart on 12 March 1917 with full honours and 10,000 people paid their last respects. During the service two Zeppelins, draped in solid black and flying funeral flags, hovered overhead and then dropped flowers as the casket was lowered into the grave.[3]

In Germany, celebrations of the centenary of Count Zeppelin's death were muted. A Zeppelin NT flew over the Count's grave, coming down to a height of fifty metres over the seventy-strong crowd. His great grandson, Albrecht, gave a speech that not only celebrated the triumphs of his great grandfather's invention, but recognised and regretted the human cost in its development and use as a weapon in the First World War.

By October and November 1918 the German High Seas Fleet was in the throes of a rebellion and soldiers' and sailors' councils assumed control with the Zeppelin

---

3. Lehmann & Mingos, op. cit., p.147.

Graf Zeppelin
† 8. März 1917

A typical postcard issued to commemorate the death of the 78-year-old Count.

L64 remained intact at the end of the war and was handed over to Britain as part of German reparations. It was flown to Pulham Airship Station on 22 June 1920 but the airship, which had seen active service, was never to fly again.

bases guarded by the sailors' soviet. Two days before the Armistice was signed the Zeppelins were deflated and left suspended by ropes from the roof trusses with resting blocks beneath.

On 23 June 1919, five days before the Treaty of Versailles was signed, many flight crews destroyed the Zeppelins in their sheds, letting the giant structures crash down onto the concrete floors. This followed the example of the German fleet, which had been scuttled two days before in Scapa Flow, and prevented delivery of the airships to the Allies or, perhaps, from falling into the hands of the revolutionary government.

This was an ignominious end to the dramatic part played in the war by the 'children' of Count Zeppelin's genius. However, the Zeppelin would rise again as a commercial vessel, gracing the skies of the world. It had prowled the night skies during the war, carrying with it an air of mystery. There was no mystery about the movement or the mechanism of the aeroplanes that followed and it is the legacy of the Zeppelin which is still being talked about over one hundred years later.

Select Bibliography

Bennett, Leon, *Churchill's War Against the Zeppelin 1914–18* (Helion & Company, Solihull, 2015)

Buttlar-Brandenfels, Freiherr Treusch von, *Zeppelins Over England* (George G. Harrap & Co., London, 1931)

Castle, H.G., *Fire Over England, The German Raids of World War I* (Leo Cooper in association with Secker & Warburg, London, 1982)

Castle, Ian, *The First Blitz – Bombing London in the First World War* (Osprey Publishing, Oxford 2015)

——, *Zeppelin Onslaught The Forgotten Blitz 1914–1915* (Frontline Books, Barnsley, 2018)

Charlton, Air Commodore L.E.O. Charlton, *War Over England* (Longmans, Green and Co., London. 1936)

De Syon, Guillaume, *Zeppelin! Germany and the Airship, 1900–1939* (The John Hopkins University Press, Baltimore, 2002)

Ellison, Wallace, *Escapes and Adventures* (William Blackwood & Sons, Edinburgh, 1928)

Fegan, Thomas, *The 'Baby Killers' – German Air Raids on Britain in the First World War* (Leo Cooper, Barnsley 2002)

Gerard, James W., *My Four Years In Germany* (Hodder and Stoughton, London, 1927)

Gutman, Jon, *Zeppelin vs British Home Defence 1915–18* (Osprey Publishing, Oxford, 2018)

Hanson, Neil, *First Blitz* (Corgi Books, London 2009)

Holt, Tonnie and Valmai, *Till the Boys Come Home: The Picture Postcards of the First World War* (Macdonald and Jane's, London, 1977)

Laffin, John, *World War I in Postcards* (Alan Sutton Publishing, Gloucester, 1989)

Lehmann, Ernst A. & Mingos, Howard, *The Zeppelins* (J. & H. Sears & Company, New York 1927)

Marks, David, *Let The Zeppelins Come* (Amberley Publishing, Stroud 2017)

Morison, Frank, *War On Great Cities – A Study of the Facts* (Faber and Faber, London, 1937)

Morris, Captain Joseph, *The German Air Raids on Great Britain, 1914–1918* (Sampson Low, Marston & Co., London 1925, reprinted by The Naval & Military Press, Dallington, 1993)

Mowthorpe, Ces, *Sky Sailors The Story of the World's Airshipmen* (The History Press, Stroud, 2010)

Poolman, Kenneth, *Zeppelins Over England* (Evans Brothers, London, 1960)

Robinson, Douglas H., *The Zeppelin in Combat* (G.T. Foulis & Co., Henley-on-Thames, 1962)

Rimmel, Raymond Laurence, *The Airship VC* (Aston Publications, Buckinghamshire, 1989)

——, *Zeppelin! A battle for war supremacy in World War I* (Conway Maritime Press, London, 1984)

——, *Zeppelin Volumes One and Two, and Zeppelins at War! 1914–1915* (Albatross Productions Ltd, Berkhamsted, 2006, 2008 and 2014)

——, *The Last Flight of The L48, The Last Flight of The L32; The Last Flight of The L31* (Albatross Productions Ltd, Berkhamsted, 2006, 2016 and 2016)

Taylor, James, *Pack Up Your Troubles. How Humorous Postcards Helped Win World War I* (Bloomsbury, London, 2016)

Welch, David, *Germany and Propaganda in World War I Pacifism, Mobilization and Total War* (I.B. Tauris & Co., London, 2014)

Whitehouse, Arch, *The Zeppelin Fighters* (New English Library, London, 1972)

Websites:
www.iancastlezeppelin.co.uk
www.airshipsonline.com
www.airships.net
www.flightglobal.com/pdfarchive/
http://www.tpa-project.info

Index

**Index of Postcard
Publishers, Artists and
Designers**